MOMENTS OF HAPPINESS

Other books in English translation by Niels Hav

God's Blue Morris
We Are Here

MOMENTS OF HAPPINESS

Poems

Niels Hav

*Translated from the Danish
by Patrick Friesen and Per Brask*

ANVIL PRESS / VANCOUVER / CANADA

Copyright © 2021 by Niels Hav
Translation Copyright © 2021 by Per Brask & Patrick Friesen
Originally published as *Øjeblikke af lykke* by Danish publisher Det Poetiske Bureaus Forlag

All rights reserved. No part of this book may be reproduced by any means without the prior written permission of the publisher, with the exception of brief passages in reviews. Any request for photocopying or other reprographic copying of any part of this book must be directed in writing to Access Copyright: The Canadian Copyright Licensing Agency, Sixty-Nine Yonge Street, Suite 1100, Toronto, Ontario, Canada, M5E 1E5.

Library and Archives Canada Cataloguing in Publication
Title: Moments of happiness / Niels Hav ; translated from the Danish by Per Brask and Patrick Friesen.
Other titles: Øjeblikke af lykke. English
Names: Hav, Niels, 1949- author. | Brask, Per, 1952- translator. | Friesen, Patrick, 1946- translator.
Description: Poems. | Translation of: Øjeblikke af lykke.
Identifiers: Canadiana 20210263377 | ISBN 9781772141870 (softcover)
Classification: LCC PT8176.18.A9 O4413 2021 | DDC 839.811/74—dc23

Cover design by Marijke Friesen
Interior by HeimatHouse

Represented in Canada by Publishers Group Canada
Distributed by Raincoast Books

The publisher gratefully acknowledges the Danish Arts Foundation for their financial assistance with the translation and publication of this book.

Danish Arts Foundation

Anvil Press Publishers Inc.
P.O. Box 3008, Main Post Office
Vancouver, B.C. V6B 3X5 Canada
www.anvilpress.com

ACKNOWLEDGEMENTS

I want to express my gratitude for the efforts of Patrick Friesen and Per Brask. This is my third book in Canada, all translated by them. Their inspired work with my poetry has enabled the poems to travel and cross boundaries.

Some of these poems first appeared in the following magazines and anthologies; *Rampike* Vol.22/No.1, Windsor, Canada; *Reading Hour* Vol 2 Issue 5, Bangalore, India; Siird en Dergisi Sayı 54, Istanbul; *Klassekampen*, Norway; *Al Mutmar*, Bagdad, Iraq; *METAMORPHOSES*, Northampton MA; *GUNU* magazine №17 Mongolia; *ECOTONE* 12 Wilmington; Ababeel, Syria; *A alma dança em seu berço,* Editora Penalux, Brazil; *Orbis* 168, West Kirby, Cheshire, UK.

TABLE OF CONTENTS

Foreword 9

PART I
The Battered Inside 13
Whose Side Am I On 15
The Funny Thing Is 17
The Tail Twirls 18
Muslims and Cyclists 19
Hypocrite 20
Rhapsody 21
Speak for Yourself 22
The Cigar Cutter 23
Assumptions 25
Must 27
It's Simply Ingenious 28
The Triumphal Entry of the Narcissists 29
All My Umbrellas Were Bought in Istanbul 30

Part II
Of Course, We Are Going to Die 33
If You're Lucky 34
Period 35
Uncommon Sense 36
In Heaven Is a Golden City 37
A Suggestion 38
Forcefully 39

A Secret 40
Dying Is Not an Employee Benefit 41
Come 42
Tintin at the Assistens Cemetery 43
A Little Encouragement 45
A Happiness Flows Through the Universe 46

Part III
A Party 49
Beneath Li Bai's Sky 51
With Charlie Chaplin in Yulin 53
Haiku 54
You Are So Stupid 55
Sleep 56
Collective Agreements 57
Okay 58
The Cranberries of Silence 59

Afterword 61

About the Author & the Translators

FOREWORD

Niels Hav was born in Lemvig, a town in the northwest part of the peninsula of Jutland, in Denmark, in 1949. This is worth mentioning because, despite the fact that for many years he has lived in a densely populated, multicultural district of Copenhagen, he has retained the down-to-earth ironical sense of humour that his birthplace is known for and melded it with the cosmopolitanism of Copenhagen and his experiences of traveling around the world as a visiting poet. This mixture has produced a poetry of deceptively straightforward language and often thought-provoking terseness.

"There are no words for it," the final line states in the poem, "If You're Lucky." There are no words for it, for the silence. Yet, it speaks. There are no words for the depth of experience, yet many words are used to suggest what it might be, what moments of happiness, sadness, loss and love, the important things, feel like in lives destined for demise. Whether in longer poems or the briefest, Hav invites a reader to consider along with him the feeling of existence, its inevitable joy, sorrow, noise, silence, not in binary terms but as mixtures. We took up his invitation as translators and now invite you to join us and him to enter the space he has created to ponder the important things.

We first translated a poem by Hav in 1990, "In Defence of Poets," and this is now the third volume of his we have worked on. Since then Hav has aged, and we have aged. Hav's poetry has always sounded a deep existential, humourous note; now it seems that with age the stakes have been raised, with an awareness of the inevitable, wistfully and with his tell-tale down-to-earth stance.

Patrick Friesen and Per Brask
Victoria and Winnipeg
August, 2021

I.

THE BATTERED INSIDE

The battered inside of the cupboard under the kitchen sink
makes me happy. Here are two honest nails
hammered into the original boards that have been there
since the apartment block was built. It's like revisiting
forgotten members of our closest family.
At some point the boards were blue; there is some leftover red
and a green pastel. The kitchen sink is new
and the counter has been raised ten centimetres. Probably
it's been renovated several times through the years.
The kitchen has remained current; there are new lamps,
electric stove, fridge and coffee maker.
But here under the sink a time warp has been allowed
its hidden existence. Here is the wash tub with the floor cloth,
the plunger and a forgotten bit of caustic soda.
Here the spider moves about undisturbed.

Maybe there's been kissing and dancing in this kitchen.
Probably there's been crying.
Happy people newly in love have prepared fragrant meals
and later cooked porridge while making sandwiches for lunch boxes.
Hungry children have stolen cookies. Laughter has resounded
in the stairwell and ropes have been skipped in the yard
while new cars were being parked outside. People moved in and out,
old ones died and were carried downstairs, newborn babies
were carried upstairs. Everything according to order —
my nameplate will also disappear from the door one day.

I get down on my knees in front of the kitchen sink
and respectfully greet the plunger, the spider
and the two honest nails.

WHOSE SIDE AM I ON?

I'm for people who have *joie de vivre* —
the ones standing outside smoking,
while the president hands out medals,
content to shiver during the applause.

The man who washes the floor and puts the chairs back.
I do not agree with the chairman,
a general secretary gives me the creeps,
have those people no self-respect?

The woman who bakes cookies for the homeless.
I'm in support of common decency.
The man who gets up in the middle of the night to deliver
newspapers on his bike, while morons piss in his bag
and call him Paki.

People who cry in their sleep at night for lack
of vitamins found only in love.
I'm for the woman collecting bottles,
and going through other people's trash
so she can give her granddaughter a trip to Rome.
The man who crosses the street to help a bewildered
boy who fell out of the nest too early.

I'm all for kindness.
I'm for him who hides his poems

in the tool drawer in the garage.
The failed ones are the most remarkable.
The one who sweeps the sidewalk including his neighbour's.
Old people who lie dying in hospitals.

I'm for him who is misunderstood
whenever he opens his mouth. The mute poets,
content with walking around mumbling to themselves,
while they take care of their work and provide for the family.
The woman the others make fun of.
The man who isn't able to manoeuver his wheelchair
and the bus driver who gets up to lend a hand.
The ones who sing in traffic. The man who makes a fool of himself.
People who move their asses.

I'm not for gang-related stockbrokers.
People who think they are the queen of heaven. Arrogant sneers.
The man who blocks other people's bank accounts.
The atmosphere in court.

I'm all for politeness, for bursting into tears
in the morning at the supermarket, common hysteria,
caring for pets, and bewitching smiles in traffic.

The man who spends seven years building a cottage
and finishes by smashing it to pieces in a rage.
That's whose side I'm on.

THE FUNNY THING IS

The funny thing is that here at Nørrebro where we live densely
packed and standing shoulder to shoulder in the bus,
everyone speaks on top of each other without concern
or with a phone held to the ear on the street, at the green grocer's,
at the supermarkets, on bicycles and even in the elevator
crammed together with strangers
who are obliged to overhear fragments of others'
intimate confessions, gleeful boasts and quarrels.
Even at the beach on a hot day in July there are no inhibitions,
as long as you know that random passersby
and anyone else on the jetty are compelled to listen in.

But on a cool summer evening walking alone in the forest
far below massive tree crowns, surrounded by silence,
the distant cooing of doves and sparrows' twittering and flitting
as the light disappears and Nature mumbles itself calm,
that's when most people feel the need to shut up.
Anyone who turns on a phone and begins to blather
will immediately sense a peculiar unease. Here no one can
stand the sound of their own naked voice
for more than a few seconds,
and the smallest lie dies in its birth.
As though the majestic trees
or unknown spirits in the underbrush
are listening.

THE TAIL TWIRLS

The boy who later became me
had a toy donkey with a tail
that could twirl when wound up.
Under its belly was a key,
you could wind up a spring with it
and the donkey's tail would twirl.
Endless fun, it amused us greatly.

Much in the public debate reminds me
of that donkey. Someone says, "burka,"
someone says, "Muslim," someone says, "terror."
And the tail twirls.

MUSLIMS AND CYCLISTS

Muslims are human beings
who live with the religion of Islam.
Some of them are cyclists
and some of them are Danes.

But not all cyclists
are Muslims
and not all Danes
are cyclists.

Yes,
This is complicated —
people are different.

HYPOCRITE

Anyone who claims, or silently
believes, that he is a mouthpiece
for Allah, God
or Buddha,
is, if possible, a worse hypocrite
than I am,
who claims a share of eternity
just because I know the price
of a diaper.

RHAPSODY

Now I will write a poem by Jan Erik Vold
about the mystery of existence —
it demands humility
but also action and protest,
jubilation, bitterness and ecstasy
to get that expressed.

In addition
a walk, language skills,
the heaviness of the melancholic —
a warm, clever and motivated person
with heavy baggage.
There are many ways of handling life.

The fundamental defect of existence
is the theme.
Less ego energy
than global energy.

Euphoria and simplicity
with or without a black border
mainly in good spirits.

Now I will embrace the globe.
We were born here
itsy, bitsy spider!

SPEAK FOR YOURSELF

Speak for yourself
said the monkey to the philosopher.

THE CIGAR CUTTER

As a confirmation gift, my grandfather gave me
a cigar cutter; the finest quality, mahogany and stainless steel.
He had great plans for me.
He himself was on the county council and the board of the bank;
he chaired the cooperative and was in the national guard —
always fond of a good cigar. He built his house in the middle of town;
there he sat in his office with a window facing the street
keeping an eye on traffic while he took care of business
and smoked his cigars.
High or low, people were greeted with calm affability
and offered a cigar from the sturdy box by the telephone.
For him the cigar cutter was a useful tool.

No doubt I've disappointed him. I never became really important;
as a rule I was too unambitious with my tobacco and was never a member
of the bank's board. I left the village with my head full of wild plans
and became one of those verbose windbags in Copenhagen.
Words are easy, but where do they lead?
The only kind of love and respect worth the effort
comes from those back home.
Which, for good reasons, is never achieved.
My grandfather died without seeing me accomplish anything at all.

The cigar cutter is still lying around here. With a little practice
you can use it to uncap beer bottles — I'm better at that.
But, in private moments, I may, at times, feel shame.

There's no use in saying, "Dear Grandfather, they've changed the world,
smoking is no longer allowed, even the bank director stands outside
in the rain now and smokes on the sly like a schoolboy."
It won't do. So silly an excuse is worth nothing,
because that's not my business. I'm my own failure.

My grandfather looks skeptically at me from his high heaven,
he cuts the tip of a Cuban, then wetting it with his lips
lights it with a table lighter molded in granite.
Mercifully he buries my confused chatter in massive clouds
of first-class smoke. He doesn't say anything,
but I know what he's thinking and deep inside myself
I have to agree with him.

ASSUMPTIONS

The unreasonable
The irresponsible
The indecent

The unreflected
The unshaven. The uncontrolled
The unsmooth
The unconditioned

The unthought through
The unworkable
The uninvited

The uncultivated
The unconquerable
The incorrect

The unfeasible
The unbearable
The illegal. The ultimate
The unpaid

The unconscionable
The impossible

The unnecessary
The unspeakable
The unnatural

The unjustifiable
Unruly & unreasonable
The unsympathetic

The undefinable

The impudent
The uncompromising
The unflagging

MUST

Must poetry be political?
Must is what we feed the chickens, my father said.
A comment on orders
and directives in general.

Poetry has no duties,
poems just have to be good.
That is why poets bite their nails,
it's not because they're starving.

When many of us still
support foreigners and listen
sceptically to the minister's cackle,
it's because it's logic: politics goes
the way of chickens.

IT'S SIMPLY INGENIOUS

Poems are in many ways different from sausages.
For instance, poems have this advantage over sausages
you can consume them —
and they are still there.
You can consume them again and again,
still, there they are.
Just like that pig from Norse mythology.

The attaché for trade at the embassy
couldn't understand that.
It simply took him by surprise.
Ingenious, he said rubbing his hands together
as though he already sat in Valhalla drinking mead.
It's simply ingenious!

THE TRIUMPHAL ENTRY OF THE NARCISSISTS

God arrives walking slowly,
dressed in rain.

The triumphal entry of the narcissists
is drowned out in the rain.

The bus is full of happy
monkeys like us.

ALL MY UMBRELLAS WERE BOUGHT IN ISTANBUL

All my umbrellas were bought in Istanbul
except the one I bought in Bursa.

Every time I go to Istanbul
I expect sunshine,
that's how I feel about Istanbul.

I forgive her —
in my mind Istanbul is bathed in sunshine.
That's why I end up standing in the rain
on Istiklal Caddesi
negotiating the price of an umbrella.
And the umbrella I bought in Bursa
I forgot in Istanbul.

There's something mystical about this,
I love those umbrellas.

II

OF COURSE, WE ARE GOING TO DIE

Of course, we are going to die,
it's the only thing we never talk about.
It's the only thing we always talk around.
Yes, we remember horses and rejoicing in a plowed field
back when God wore shorts.
Now all that is framed by car windows.
We stop at the outer edge and stand for a moment in the rest area
and listen to the bushes that are but a narrow border
of despondent trees, a little ghetto surrounded by smog
from the motorway and poison clouds from cultivated land.

Yes, somewhere in there the yellow bunting still sings
even if no one is listening any longer.
The forest floor is littered with black plastic bags full of dead things
strewn between anemones and — what the hell!
It might be that God is in a springtime mood, even if we
are here to take our leave of Nature,
on our way to the hospital to be cut open
in honour of the angels,
while everything we've ever loved or owned
turns to compost.

IF YOU'RE LUCKY

If you're lucky everything is silent.
Everyone knows it. Someone talks,
but no one says anything
because no one can say it. Finally.
It's just curious.
There are no words for it.

PERIOD

Anyway, not everything works out in the end,
complete confusion takes over —
a final gaping wonder.
Maybe it's sunlight, maybe rain,
a lacerated sky, ragged clouds,
or just winter and dirty slush.
Everyone wearing the wrong clothes,
delayed smiles drift about in the confusion,
awkward handshakes.
No one grasps what's going on.
The traffic is unconcerned…
One of those days that after all
isn't one of those days. A black hole on the calendar,
old snow, dried tears.
The parking lot is half empty.
Someone arrives carrying a bouquet
of irrevocable loneliness,
2-1 = 0

UNCOMMON SENSE

Most important is to avoid eternal things
and existential issues. Let's talk about something ordinary,
like bicycles and the rain. Or just about mosquitoes.
About how you grow sleepy when it rains all afternoon,
and you don't have to ride your bike to the beach.
Best of all is to have a tool shed with a tin roof,
or get married to a pianist playing Chopin.

Maybe we're just getting more stupid as we get older
and our common sense evaporates.
Purity of heart is to will only one thing, that we know.
That's why young people make the best soldiers
— they will only one thing at a time.
Just like mosquitoes on a rainy summer day.

IN HEAVEN IS A GOLDEN CITY

About life in heaven
we don't know much.
The snobs claim
that existence is completely
meaningless. That's up to them.

I no longer believe
everything is something I'm dreaming.
My father died many years ago
and I'm already older
than he got to be.

In heaven is a golden city,
is written on his tombstone.
Now, after a long time, I finally know
what it will say on mine,
See you up there!

A SUGGESTION

Let's make an agreement
that the two of us stay alive
like Methuselah
until we're 969.

Then we'll see what
happens next.

FORCEFULLY

Joys evaporate
and everything disappears
in a scurry.

But give me,
give me —
oh, yes, give me again
a gulp
of the wildest
happiness
straight into my heart
muscle!

A SECRET

Now when the idiotic rain carries on
and we are all busy dying
I have a desire to smoke. But smoking
is prohibited at the airport in Beograd.
I asked one of the employees for advice.
"Smoking kills," he said.
"Yes," I said, "but it turns out
that non-smokers die, too."

"Let me tell you a secret,"
he said. "Go to gate A6,
below that, there's a washroom.
That's where we smoke."

I followed his directions,
they worked out. I savoured the secret
joy of doing something prohibited.
Why should I cheat readers of poetry
out of useful info — poetry is already
so full of esoteric wisdom.

DYING IS NOT AN EMPLOYEE BENEFIT

People die wherever it occurs to them,
in traffic, on a sidewalk, during a war.
Spontaneous deaths happen all day long.

Most people reasonably prefer
to die in their spare time, that way
avoiding any loss of pay.

Anyone who dies immediately loses
their entitlement to mileage, overtime pay
and per diems — at a time when they really

need it. It's costly to live,
but dying, too, is usually
bad business.

COME

Come let us walk over
and sit sheltered by the dike
on a dry April day, the sun
luring lice and mosquitoes
out from the tree's dead bark.

Touch the earth with your ass
and feel how grass and weeds
tingle merrily
even on this overlooked spot
in a corner of the globe.

Lift a stone and greet worms
and centipedes. One day, soon,
when this wild ember is dead
the earth's microorganisms will
hungrily receive your flesh.

Good, despite fear and snot,
something works! Rest your knees
sit here sheltered and satisfy your eyes
on mosquitoes and lice. There's
still flesh on your bones.

TINTIN AT THE ASSISTENS CEMETERY

Last time I met Tintin
he was sitting in the Assistens Cemetery.
I was on my bicycle, we greeted each other,
but I didn't stop —
I wasn't aware that this
was the last time I'd see him.
Now and then we would chat a little
when we met by the lakes
or at Ravnsborggade. He was always in the company
of women whom he entertained
charmingly, fencing with his cane
and commenting on traffic.

Now he was sitting alone, no women or anyone else with him.
When you reach your nineties
many of your buddies have already crawled into their coffins.
He looked a little lost, possibly he was here
to study the route before his last trip.
It was September, birds flew silently about.

"Hi, Palle," I called from my bicycle.
He looked up, eyes sparkling,
then he lifted his cane.
"Hi, hi," he yelled and waved.
That was the last time I saw Tintin.

(At the age of 15, Palle Huld (1912-2010) won the *Politiken* (newspaper) contest to travel around the world in 44 days in celebration of the centenary of the birth of Jules Verne. He returned to an enthusiastic reception and later wrote the book, *Around the World with Palle in 44 Days*. It was translated into many languages and it inspired Hergé to create the character Tintin).

A LITTLE ENCOURAGEMENT

I woke up and felt awful
about myself
all morning. Until I opened the newspaper
and read the obituaries —
then I felt better.

Apparently
at least I hadn't died
recently.

A HAPPINESS FLOWS THROUGH THE UNIVERSE

The furniture is falling apart
clothes unravel, shoes wobble — it is April.
On a luscious evening we go for a walk along the lakes
and study the buds on the chestnut trees
as we talk alternately of plans for the summer
and of the winter's dead. Where did they go?

Children wheel by, cheering on new bicycles,
joys racing at a clip.
...
Sorrow comes limping
like an invalid.

As darkness descends we silently greet the dead
standing in the shadows under the chestnut trees
and along house fronts where darkness imperceptibly
creeps up from basements.
Dead leaves from last year have blown together
under bushes, on their way into the earth.

Confidently we take each other's hand — a happiness
flows through the universe.

III

A PARTY

I went for a walk in Wenling in the late afternoon, the temperature hovering around zero. Then it began to snow. I felt utterly dark inside. Along potholed sidewalks there were stalls and street kitchens and a bustle of Chinese people of all ages, a traffic jam of pedestrians, cars, bicycles and mopeds. It snowed; large wet flakes came densely down from the gray sky. Winter had arrived in Wenling. Here and there clumps of men sat around braziers playing cards while snow fell over the city's potholed streets. I wandered, I stood and watched. A big snowfall had arrived on the Chinese continent.

I stopped at a brazier and greeted the card players, joyful people, women and children scurrying about doing chores. I was heartily welcomed, offered tea, shown a stool. We couldn't speak together, because I don't know Chinese, but we laughed together. It snowed. We drank tea and studied the cards. The men laughed at each other's jokes and at my awkward presence. I had dropped from another planet. It snowed, the slushy street became white meringue traversed by black tracks from cars and mopeds. The tea was spicy and strong, hot air rose from the brazier. We laughed together. They laughed at me, I laughed with them, about my idiotic travels here and there. I don't think they felt poor, they have telephones, television, a bed. They live in simple rooms surrounded by family and friends. Maybe they have some small longing, a wild dream and a few secrets, what do I know? Undoubtedly, they saw me as a harmless fool. A wretch perhaps, in my failed homelessness; I didn't even recognize the cards. But they allowed me to sit with them while winter arrived in Wenling. I was permitted to warm up by their fire, to recover, to be a human being in any case. We laughed, we drank tea, we smoked, it snowed; it was a party.

BENEATH LI BAI'S SKY

We are nomads, just like you —
This evening I sit in the doorway dreaming,
I don't want to go in, I don't want to go out —
I stare at your old moon,
your old moon stares at me
in the dark, insects play an ancient concert
far away the mountains speculate

On the motorways traffic roars,
anxiety hides in skyscrapers,
the soul shivers in an overheated office
and rage glows in ashes from burned-out visions

The dead have returned to their homelands
the living are still on the move
The driver having neither route nor direction is lost
a minor personal disaster, we empathize with him —
when humanity and all the world have lost the way
no one notices

This evening, we are in Zaoyang,
I sit in the doorway dreaming
Zaoyang is a beautiful city, real people live here,
they care about right and wrong and chasing happiness —
the universe is pervaded by insatiable longing
Hello Li Bai, where are you?

I sit alone beneath your sky in Zaoyang
drinking your wine

WITH CHARLIE CHAPLIN IN YULIN

It is said that the Great Wall of China
can be seen from the moon —
That's complicated and expensive to verify,
but it is certain that the moon can be seen
from the Great Wall

When Charlie Chaplin meets Genghis Khan someday in Yulin
they can stand on the Great Wall or in the watchtower
studying the moon as they exchange values

"The greatest happiness is to triumph over your enemies,
rob them and take their wives and daughters in your arms,"
says Genghis Khan
"I'm sorry but I don't want to be an emperor," Chaplin replies,
"that's not my business. I want to live in other people's happiness"

As the moon is a metaphor for love and longing
the Great Wall is a metaphor for the powerlessness
of empire-builders, all empires expire

Today Genghis Khan is a Mongolian barbecue
and Charlie Chaplin is dead. God created this world
with a good sense of humour; most of our glorious history
is but a big joke, so let's not forget to laugh.

HAIKU

My thoughts are abuzz
like bluebottles around shit.
Now I need a bath.

YOU ARE SO STUPID

You are really stupid
if you trick yourself
into believing that you are smarter
than the limping pedestrian
who, howling in a rage,
attacks himself with curses
and swear words because he forgot
his keys, his name
even his address.

You do know where he lives.
That's your shoes he's wearing.
That's you he's calling for,
that's your name on the door.
Come on, let's go home now.

SLEEP

Walk quietly, speak softly
never wake someone sleeping
for no good reason. Sleep
is holy!

The most beautiful part of life
happens while sleeping,
there I have often met wonderful
women. We melted together
in blessed harmony
and became completed beings.

I have been to every possible place
in dreams and always as myself.
In the daytime — when I'm awake —
I sometimes imagine
that I'm someone else,
but never at night,
in dreams I am me.

COLLECTIVE AGREEMENTS

In the mornings I prefer to write.
In the afternoons I prefer to read interesting books
or go for a walk.
In the evenings I am with my family.
Night shifts are not for me.
Find someone else.

OKAY

Whenever the others pretend
they don't see you,
it's not because they don't see you —
they just feel like pretending
that they don't see you.
Isn't that okay?

THE CRANBERRIES OF SILENCE

How long can you shut up
before you become *stum*?

How long can you blather
before you become *dum*?

AFTERWORD

I was born on the west coast of Denmark, far from the capital where I live today. In a sense I'm a newcomer here, like the Arabs, Pakistani, and Turkish immigrants living in my neighbourhood. I spoke a rural dialect when I was a kid. Of course I belong to the literary landscape in Denmark, but I never had the feeling of belonging to any generation or movement in Danish poetry. I arrived with completely different experiences than the urban poets. I remember what joy it was when I first came across poems by Ted Hughes and Seamus Heaney, for example. They wrote in a larger space than the urban turf and on experiences with nature and animals which I could immediately recognize. Today I am a city dove and I feel at home in Copenhagen, but maybe it's still there I stand, a kind of outsider who also has other relationships and belongs in other contexts.

Poetry is, of course, for everyone; poems are addressed to just about anyone. But I am talking about the profession, the craft, the daily practice of writing poetry. It requires courage and stamina to work in this field. And a willingness to renounce private lyricism and unbridled emotionalism, which always threatens to drown poetry. The characteristic of good poets is all the bad poems they never write. What I mean is: poetry contains elements of music and fun, but not only that. Time passes, we live and die. The world is on fire. Politics, bombs, ideology and religion ravaging the globe.

This is what the adults are talking about — and at its innermost core the challenge for art is to join this conversation. To find out and understand what's going on, and if possible to say things as they are. So, yes, poetry — the profession — is not for wimps. You have to face yourself and look reality, God, whatever that is, directly in the eyes. Poetry's first duty is to be an intimate talk with the single reader about the deepest mysteries of existence.

But if a poem is to be of interest to anyone other than the poet, it must in some sense be emblematic. When I write a poem about my Dad, for example, the poem must be so exemplary that the reader can move in and take over the poem and be there with their own father. I'm not oiling the reader with my private feelings and reflections — then it would just be about me. The poem must be designed, or developed, so that the reader can feel at home there with their personal thoughts and feelings and make the words their own. Now they belong to them. In the end my personal experiences are completely unimportant, I have written the poem and handed it over to the reader, to everyone. My father never got a passport, but the poem has been read on stage in China and Dubai, and it seems to work also in Arabic and Chinese. Everybody has a father.

Poetry is often a futile activity. I'm sure most poets know the feeling. My wife is a concert pianist, every morning she sits down at the piano, and I go to my office. Often nothing happens. I am there, the words are there, and nothing happens. On a good day my confusion and doubts may lead to a poem. It is the daily practice, and the contact with the written material, which sometimes brings electricity to language and lets the words sparkle. I write slowly or in spurts, but things are often left for a while before they are published. They lie there and mature. And sometimes, perhaps much later, I look at the material again and suddenly realize that there it is: this is a poem. When that happens, it is because the text holds surprises even for me. So the process is still somewhat of a mystery. A new poem is a gift; it can happen suddenly on the street, in traffic, while you take care of daily chores, a little epiphany. But a good poem is rarer than a dead badger on the freeway or a UFO.

— Niels Hav,
Copenhagen

Based on an interview with Dutch magazine Meander.

About the Author

Niels Hav is a Danish poet, his books have been translated into Portuguese, Arabic, Turkish, Dutch, and Farsi. He has travelled widely in Europe, Asia, Africa, North and South America. In Canada, he has attended the Vancouver International Readers & Writers Festival and other festivals. About his previous book, Frank Hugus said in *The Literary Review* "...Niels Hav's *We Are Here* brings to us a selection from the works of one of Denmark's most talented living poets and is all the more welcome for that reason...." *Moments of Happiness* is Niels Hav's third book published in Canada.

About the Translators

Per Brask has published three books of poetry and five volumes of co-translations of poetry from Denmark with Patrick Friesen. He lives in Winnipeg.

Patrick Friesen has published more than a dozen books of poetry, a book of essays, and has co-translated, with Per Brask, five books of Danish poetry, including *Frayed Opus for Strings & Wind Instruments* by Ulrikka Gernes, which was nominated for the Griffin Poetry Prize in 2016. Patrick's most recent title is *Outlasting the Weather: Selected and New Poems 1994-2020*. He lives in Victoria, BC.